I can feel it in my roots;
I gave birth, in a nightmare,
to unlovable things.
They breed in my belly;
tiny birthdays, every day.
I am the undead mother to
every single bit
of black
in this skin prison
my lovers
have choked on.

also by j.r. rogue

Novels
Background Music
Burning Muses

Poetry
La Douleur Exquise
An Open Suitcase & New Blue Tears
Rouge
Le Chant Des Sirènes
Letters to the Moon
Secrets We Told The City
w/Kat Savage
Exits, Desires, & Slow Fires

All Of My Bullshit Truths: Collected Poems

Tell Me Where It Hurts

poems

j.r. rogue

For the Caged Birds.
If I can sing, so can you.

Tell Me Where It Hurts

Tell me where it hurts.
Deep in your dermis?

This world is full of victim shaming/
blaming/DEGRADING

& you can't quit scratching at that spot just
above your ruby highways & back alleys.

Where your blood slithers & whispers
you brought this upon yourself.

Tell me where it hurts.
Deep in your ribcages?

I can see them there;
the confessions caged inside.

I hear them singing
but you can't bear to listen.

I'm here to tell you
the truth that's roaring in the
river raging inside of you.

Shake the shame from your skin.
You did nothing wrong.

Circus 2005

Spring. This life is n e w for you. Re-
branding starts now. *Tick tock;* the clock
exhales midnight & new beginnings laugh
track off your tongues.

She said *the us we were cannot survive the rest of
Winter.* So you kissed her & whispered lies
into her hair. You did not know. You were
so skilled at slipping knives in your own
back, being shocked by it all.

Her fingernails, peppermint.
You cannot throw away your addict lips.
She told you some poet warned her of
making h o m e s out of human beings, she
screamed to you that they were fools, & she
begged you not to do the same to her.

But you have. You cannot undo.

Her birthday is carved into the tree in your
backyard. You lit a candle & took her there
at Midnight & new beginnings laughed
tracked off your tongue.
She cupped them to her chin & tried to
inhale them.

Summer. Some shine for Tuesday Morning.
You changed your tie 27 times
this week to match her eyes.
They roll with the weather, with the pills at
standing ovation on the bottom shelf of the
medicine cabinet. They greet you every
morning she does not.

You threw away your forfeit vocabulary in
2004. You don't have words for this day. For
her day. For tomorrow. Her phone facing
down tells more truth than she can
strangle.You will n o t q u i t.

On the third Monday this week you found
her weeping into her cereal bowl over a
man she never knew whose death has
washed upon the shore of the 6 o'clock
news.
I'm dying every day, look at me.
It's too early for this. New beginnings, my dear.

You touch the tears on her cheek & think I
want to be the reason she f e e l s.
She rolls with the weather, & I am nothing,
the vane spinning in her wind.

Fall. She wants to make love so often you
divorced a steady pulse. The bedposts are
bruised, you bought them a drink &
laughed at your fortune.

She is alive again.

She fingered your red hair & told you she
never thought a ginger lover could make
her come home.

Her tongue is your favorite wine. She didn't
show up for your last two dates. You found
her at home once,

laughing to your favorite Steve Martin
movie, wondering why you had missed the
beginning,

next in her panties, liquid idle ankles
hanging from the backyard swing, in
cahoots with her phone, with a phantom,

one finger, a warning, to stay away as she
plotted & preened to someone she says she
never knew.

Winter. You are studying her.

Behind the spine of her books
& behind the curtain of the shower, &
behind the eye of the door, as she undresses
from the day

& brushes her teeth & unwinds the slow
coil of society's expectations from her neck,
careful not to shake the rattle.

You made her cum twice this week, she
doesn't know you shaved your beard.

The office temp brushed your shoulder, she
looked you in the eye & you felt a shiver.

Not this year, repeat repeat repeat it again…

Your heart is beating in a burning building.
She asked you not to do that to her.

But you have.
You cannot undo. You don't want to.

You tell her *the us we are cannot survive the rest
of Winter.*

Five Minutes Baby

His voice is like a beating drum
& I want him to hum
between my thighs.
He is a prize I need to win
because 80 years tastes
bitter in this bite of mine.

His sex means
the crown balances nicely,
though it doesn't fit.
It precariously balances
on the head he
pats as he grabs
his scuffed boots
& takes my sex sweat with him.

Give me five minutes
& I will
show you just how deep you can fall into
my nothingness.

Give me five minutes & I will
show you just how easy it is to unlove me.

Impersonal Ad

No one tells you how to grieve the
monsters.
No one tells you how
to make tears
manifest into daggers,
let them somersault into your own back.

Your self-betrayal
must be rewarded in unkind.

At 4 am they found me
chained to a neon lover.
I needed more
than the cards
carrying condolences
stacked *so sorry* high on my night stand.

The zombie crowd
fumbling after his hearse
flayed me alive with switchblade eyes.

They saw the billboard
advertising my
unique skills.

WORST DAUGHTER ALIVE! BLAME
DEVOURER! GUARANTEED TO LET

YOU CUT HER OPEN!
POUR YOUR ACID INSIDE! MONEY
BACK GUARANTEE!

At 5 am they found me
with slit wrists
& Society's open gullet,

so they smiled.

I Died but Attended The Funeral

I attended a funeral,
too many
years ago.

My tenderness was
too young,
to be ripped
away,
so soon.

I mourn her;
& on Spring days,
when I see the
gentle flutter
of a Blue Jay's
wings,

I hope
that somewhere,
she is
smiling.

"I feel like because I'm able to
cope seemingly well on the outside with my
issues that when an instance comes up that
brings out the darkness, no one gets it."

–Danielle Kinder

Hereditary Blues

This disease is in our blood.
I try to deny it.
I can't.
I was slapped in the face with it

once again tonight.
This depression drips from our eyes
behind closed doors.

We have become
damn good at fooling others.
We paint happy faces on &
check strings

attached to limbs
attached to vocal chords
attached to lips
attached to firm hand shakes

& half assed hugs.
We dance the way others do;
day in, day out.
We play the part of happy-go-lucky little
grownups.

Inside, we dream of the highs.
The days painted with

cotton candy blues & faces turned away
from the
low
low
lows
coming in too soon.

Sternum Scars & Secrets

High collars & higher heels.
Hide it all
from the sleepwalkers
& the city
sinners
panhandling
for your kiss
& your hand
& your one-night stand
tickets.

Keeps the lights low
& your scars won't
show.

Keep the sex rough
& your secrets
won't know
you fucked them over
& stood them
up again.

Have You Seen This Person?

I become a missing person
in the middle of conversations.
I'm not interested in your
story unless your
face frowns at the exact moment
mine falls.
Someone stole my light so
now I sneak into your
heart to snatch yours.
I shove it in my ebony eyeholes
& pray that it'll stay.
Please,
I implore you,
look inside my insides.
Do you see ink
where crimson
should roar?
Is the sea inside
my belly black as night?
I admit,
I don't know who I am,
anymore.

Lies Liars Tell

You move to small little
towns to raise
small little families
where it's safe & small,
& nothing bad happens,
nothing at all.

But just two months ago,
at the gas station
around the corner, a man
forced the clerk out
at knife point & made her
drive his car to
her own nightmare.

Now the newspaper tells me
this rapist lives two streets
over from me
& my small blue house.

So, please tell me you have
found a safe place,

so that I can tell you
that is a lie.

Wet Pavement

My parents gave me an ordinary name. It
was in fashion. I always found myself
surrounded by a sea of me. My parents
never let me believe I was ordinary, though.

They placed crowns on my head &
whispered adorations into my ears. Despite
their efforts, I always felt stuck to the
background; drowning in the faceless girls

wearing my name. My life feels like a car
crash; sort of like the one I found myself in
at seventeen-years-old when the only sound
heard that night was the wet

smack of pavement beneath my converse as
I ran home, away from the fire & sirens &
casualties of my fickle ways, fused to the
passenger seat.

My first kiss was on a worn down leather
couch. I pull it out on Sundays that need to
be cried in. I didn't move, I lay there, stoic
& dissolving. He pressed his lips to me

& I was a cold dead fish. I'm not sure why
he tried again. *They always try again.* I like
to lay that kiss on my hardwood floors &
pull out the filet knife while Creep plays

softly from my record player. I try to see
what's inside. I was taught to lie still from a
young age, ah yes, I see it now. I put the kiss
back in its box once the waste bin fills

up with any slivers of shock white
innocence I've managed to grow back. My
last first kiss was on a Tuesday. I think it
was the 4th of July but I'm always forgetting

magic, clichés, & shit like that. He made
love to the vodka, the vengeance in my
mouth. I wore a suit of armor, ruby rebound
glasses. I placed a little fire in my

hair so I wouldn't drown in a sea of girls
wearing the same lace. Sometimes I think of
him; he is forgettable, but that girl isn't.

Now, outside the suburban streets are dark.
The screaming house across the asphalt is
silent for once. They've cupped their ears to

the door, listening for the sound of my feet on wet pavement.

Unfiltered Intimacy

You're so very suppliant, sincere. My ear
finds your chest & I listen to
a screenplay of the life I want
us to have. *A Sunday
Special.*

Who gifted you those hands? Where did you
get them? Was that your
mother? Your father? I'd like
to

send them a thank you note. Something to
express my gratitude. They're
resurrecting. They're
miracles. You use my armor
as a

cutting board, placing all the tender bits you
know I own gently against
my will power. Slicing them
open. You press me

against you, close, one leg over yours, one
arm over your chest. "When
we are like this, skin to skin,
I can hear you." You see

the girl behind the filters & the makeup &
           the false bravado & the dark
           slimming colors. You see the
           girl behind the lies I tell;

I am sane, I am normal, no one ever broke
           me. You see the girl behind
           the words & the metaphors &
           the image. You see me.

The silence I wear frightens other men. I can
           see it in their sideways
           glances & the way they kiss
           me, pulling me nearer.

Hand prints on hipbones - desperation. They
           fear the homes & hearts &
           worlds I retreat into; not you.
           You see me.

Nothing has ever been so terrifying.

He Wants To Be a Poem

He read my words & the seduction
snuck inside of him.
Now he's drawing hearts around my name
& painting himself in a way that he
was never meant to be.

He molds himself after every
'he' he sees
in every stanza
in every metaphor
in every letter I pen.

He wants to be a poem
so he tries to fuck me like I am
glass & daisies; like I will break apart
in his hands
because he thinks he knows me now.

He's consumed my phrases &
smeared his eyelids with what he
sees of my soul.

He wants to be a poem;
so I break him just like the rest.

Open Books & Open Wounds

My screams ricochet
off the walls in my veins.
Topsy turvy,
descending, white knuckled,
gripped,
grasping for the escape hatch.

They bolted &
took me down.

My tongue is a
double edged sword.

"Why are you so open with your life?"

Burgundy shimmies her
dress down to bruised rose.
You're half a victim if
you're now exposed.
Your hurt won't bring
half the cash.

You're a cast out.
Even the statistical
kids skip off to cliques.

"It's so good to see you're moving on now."

"Just once it would be nice to be asked if I'm okay and I could be able to say no. I'm not. I'll never be okay. People never want to hear the sad, tormented side of the girl who's always happy and laughing."

–*Catye Nutt*

Oh, Esther

I fear I'm going the Esther-Greenwood-way.
I'm dizzy & blind to
my own pale fingers
wrapped around my often
quiet & modest throat.

I've always had this strange fear of
swallowing
my own tongue,
yet I still speak to you.
Every fraction of faltering gets brushed
aside a little more
as I pour myself out.

I fear I'll push
& pull
& pummel
my non-fiction until it is
        something you deem edible.

I'm choking on my self-sabotage.
I'm choking on my obsession with you.

Recalculating

The moon, how she seduces.
The way she
keeps me company
so sporadically, is such a sad little shame.

You've taken to the couch,
again.
Again again, we spiral.

I am venom veins. Too heavy.
I shall not spill them
with your apologies.
They fall forth.

You've taken to the couch,
& I've curled up with maps—
crinkling like avalanches
down the staircase.

Will you hear me?
I am wide eyed & suffering.
Is it not enough?

I curl up with maps-
my future, far from you.

I see it now.

The day your suitcase falls so heavy
from your hands
behind a new door;
where love tastes not of ugly things.

Where you don't have to
ache for me anymore.

Begin Here

at the root of it
humid nights
& an off
center mirror

I can't step
into bathrooms
without

murdering
my bottom lip
for an hour

he's in the grave

somersaulting
until winter

we buried
his false faces
there

I am haunted by
his true one

Bullseye

Daddy issues & dark locks,
storming my shoulders.
X marks the spot
over my heart.

(Stop talking about it.)
(No one cares.)

Shall I write it on my jawline?

Bullseye.

Will the sticky words
clash with my blouse, my heels,
& my self-loathing?
The universe is busy tonight,
but everyone will notice.
Flaws love to dance in
funhouse mirrors.

The *hypothetical me*
wears these tarnished
knees with a smile.

I shower in tequila shots
& play chicken with
my reflection

in the bathroom glass.

(They care, but they're scared.)

Fishing

I went fishing
down by the
water,
where I
often drown
happily-ever-after's,
with an
old lover.

He offered
sage advice for
my train-wreck-life,
& I offered
my fidelity on
a rusty
truck bed.

I have to spend
something like
forever
with this
long false laugh
that is falling
from
my traitor tongue.

He says he can't

spend the night warm
between the thighs

of a woman
who confuses suicide
notes with romance.

Collect Calls & Cries

You will never trust phone booths.
Superman may change into his
red & blue there,
but your mother
clutched a dingy
dangling receiver
on an ink black night
inside of one
after a stranger
violenced his way inside of her.

You will never trust.

Self-Harm

Shit-fathers love last chances.
Phone calls carrying tears
& cancer to excuse the damage done.
I let you forgive him because
the sickness had him.

It was eating his bones
& my guilt was
infesting my marrow.

I let the world pity him for a bit
& I choked on it.

self-harm

Summer of 2012 brought news
of a new victim.

I wear a suit of flesh
with kin in pain

I wonder if she damned
him
or forgave him because
they share a family name.

No one likes a victim's tale.

Show you a survivor's tale
or you'll forget me?

"No matter how much therapy you've had
it never really goes away. It's like living in
constant fight or flight mode; sometimes
you can turn it off,
and sometimes you can't."

–Gabriela Tovar

Embalmed Decay

Bathe me in dirt.
I am not.
I am not a pretty thing.
I am the dead you left behind.

I hope the worms
make a meal of you.

I hope your name
is gone, that the
weather rips
away at
your headstone,
before
our hands grow
knobby
& our children
become grand.

You are the worst of
this world.
A thief in broad daylight.

Innocent children,
robbed
of laughter lines & sanity.

I hope to hold the hands
of every little girl
you left broken.

Baptism

When I was eight-years-old
I took a bubble bath.
I sunk down & let the
warm water & suds devour me.

I thought of all my moving parts below
the surface.
What they were meant for.
What they could do.
What men would love me for them.

I didn't think about my scraped knee
from falling off my bicycle.

I didn't think about the bruise on my arm
from falling out of the
neighbors
large tire swing.

I didn't think about the things my body was
truly meant for when I was
eight-years-old.
I lost time.
I lost myself.

When will I come back?

He Haunts

A dead man
is playing the violin
in the corner of my room again.

He wants me to remember
the color purple
& the bruises that will never fade
on my lungs.

I unstitched my mouth,
ripped my voice from
his wrecking hands.

I shoved it down my
coward throat,
let my mother know
she once loved
a monster.

I let her know it
wasn't her fault
& we all
wear blind eyes
from time to time.

Feather Cages

John Smith would never hurt her.

There are too many Johns in the world,
& too many Pocahontas costumes
on All Hollows' Eve.

She locks herself away when
the neighbors set pumpkins
on their doorsteps.
No one comes to hers.

When she was seven she wanted
to explore a new world.
& he gave her one.

He watched her every Thursday
when her mother worked late
at the Crazy Horse Pawn Shop.

They watched Disney movies
& played hide & seek.
They played make believe &
one night he played with her
boundaries
while a cartoon
droned in the background &
she wore her new Halloween costume.

One night that Indian princess sang
& she sobbed
& she never made a sound.

Rx for the Reverberations

I carry a Richter scale in
my pocket.
I'm still feeling vibrations
from '93.
I'll get a handle on this yet.
Allow me, please, a moment
to feel feelings I'm not allowed to.

Stockholm Syndrome
& his memory.
My cell is *chirp chirping* through the day.

I signed my name down for twice
a month on Thursdays.
A comfy pillow & a chaise lounge.
Will it be like the movies?
I'll talk to the walls
& the stranger in
the room will paint
my symptoms on
a fresh legal pad
& write me
a prescription for closure.

My childhood looked best in the
dingy mirror above my vanity.

My lover pinned my hands behind
my back & broke the glass.

I can't go back.

Stepford

Once or twice a year on Sundays
you'll catch me on the front porch of my
little blue house on 6th & Monroe.

I'll have a mug in
my hand & a smile
on my face. My hand will rise &
fall as my neighbors pass by.
My voice will offer a pleasant hello.

But the thing is, if you come too close,
you'll see my truth.

The cup is empty.
My eyes too.

See, from time to time I like
to pretend just like you.

"What do I want people to ask me?
'Do I forgive them.'
What I wish people would say?
'I'm so sorry I didn't believe you.'"

–*Angela Wallace*

Weathervanes & Paper Planes

At the top of our roof,
sits a weathervane.
I can see it from here.
Spring has not yet given birth.

I often escape to
this tree house
away from the secret
swallowing swelling walls I live in,
away from night sweats
& hidden scars.

Within these branches,
I can set them free.
A child should not wear
such heavy shoulders,
slouching towards the soil.

I remain, for hours,
seated at that old schoolhouse desk.
I write myself away.
I write myself with fins for sea swimming
& black wings for night diving.

I   write
until dusk has fallen,
& I am being called in for supper

where we will say grace, & I will pray to a
God that does not answer me;
where I smile pretty & perfect
& will
myself undamaged.

My fantasies are
folded into paper planes.
They fly away the way I wish to.

Seraphina's Song

I set the first story bathroom
on fire when I was nine-years-old.
I still have a scar on my wrist.

I tried to put it out
when I thought about my mother mourning
her favorite porcelain sink,
the first place she bathed me in.

I still can't step on tile with my bare feet.
I jump from showers to rugs to hallways.

That first story bathroom
was the first muse that
broke me.

I set it on fire while my
grandparents shopped for
sugar & cinnamon & vanilla
to bake my birthday cake.

While my mother pulled
fresh calla lilies from the
garden because she knows I love them so.

I threw my grandmother's
curling iron in the trash.

They blamed it on that.

I never took baths there again,
& I still sleep with a lighter
beneath my pillow.

He never touched me again.

The Butterfly Effect

His father named him Avery on the second
Tuesday of November, some
thirty odd years ago.

He cried his first cry & his mother smiled.
"Avery," his father said.
Simple.
Done.
No need for discussion.
He had a name & a place.

He escaped home early
& grew to be a worker.
His hands formed worn spots &
his brow was always furrowed.
He clipped coupons & turned
the lights off as he left each room.
His wallet was always fat
& he & his lady dined in.

He had a safe full of guns.
He cleaned them in front of his lover.
"This one isn't legal in this state,
so don't tell anyone I have it,"
he grinned & winked;
she loved being in on the secret.

He kept his ruining tools in plain sight.
His guns, his hands, his mouth.
He was a drug.
She would never leave.

She left him with her little boy
every other Sunday,
as she ran the register at
Casey's General store on 6th & Washington.

We forget little boys lose innocence
in low lighting as church bells ring &
choir members wipe their brows
& praise the Lord;
as patterns repeat &
lips are stitched.

Ashes

There are ashes
raining outside
my third story window.
They say they want
to teach me about fire—
about me.

They whisper as they
feather down & blanket West 4th Street.
They say they want me to
tip toe through their canvas,
& paint a pretty picture.

They say they'll show me
the art my cruelty creates,
one day.

Ribcaged Confessions

I name my ribs every night
before I go to sleep.
I name them
& I curse them
& I tell them
I never loved them.

For they hide my heart
&
everything I long to say
in this world
lies within them.

Curtain Call

I'm trying to figure out a way
to unmake you from a poem.

I'm looking for the wires in your hair, for
the spark you wear. I fiction-fuck you after
one glass of wine. It doesn't take much,
really.

I was nineteen, green, wearing sternum scars
& naked thighs. You had hair past your
breast bone, fashioned a lopsided smile into
snake-snap-traps.

I'm trying to figure out a way
to unmake you from my memory.

You caught me with my mouth open &
every morning since I've tried to untaste
you. We both woke up that day feeling a
desire to be false & hip & cliché; the
mulberry accent wall at that odd named cafe
was the backdrop for your grand entrance to
my life, the meet-cute.

Your eyes introduced you before your lips
parted.
You were trying to figure out a way

to unmake yourself from this life.

When you paid for my mint tea & sesame
muffin, your prescription receipts & recipes
for getting better slipped out a bit, you were
off guard, my smile does that.

Sternum scars & no defense. The fresh start.
The sinful part was I didn't have to tell you
what had happened to me, you coaxed it
from me less than a week later. You wanted
to hear it, you wanted to taste it from my
lips, though you knew.

I'm trying to figure out a way
to unmake you from my life.

It took me twenty-seven months & fifteen
days to pick up my pen again. I wrote traitor
poetry two weeks ago. I said I was over you
then this shit poured from my eyes & lips &
dripped onto conspirator pages.

Some days the sheets stayed white, blinding
me like the white of your eyes, the flash of
your smile, the scent of our bed. I debated
waiving it in the air, a white flag substitute,

a Siamese twin to every man I've let into my
room since.

My mother called me today. *Have you heard
the news?* she asked. More gossip & small
town legends, I knew that's what she had for
me. I can't escape them, or you, here in this
city, it seems.

No, not today. I've been listening to your
favorite song on repeat since lunch, five
glasses past the one I need to get your naked
ghost into my head.

*You've finally figured out a way
to unmake yourself from your own life.*

You Can Get Better If You Try

This is where I leave you.
Can't you see?
My eyes no longer make love.
I'm clenched & carved up for you.

"I just think so many people use depression
as an excuse..."

Make a steady line down the center.
I'm sinking but I'm pretty.
Don't let them forget I'm pretty.
I want the bile to be beautiful for them.

"I just think you fantasize that you own that
word. That no one else is allowed to be as
sad as you."

I imagine you came here for love,
but I'm spent.
I left it on Ferro Avenue.
I tucked it beneath my pillow
with that stubborn molar.

I hoped the fairy thief
in the night would be gentle.
I ran out of gifts to give.

"It's because something bad happened to
you. You weren't born this way. So I just
think you can get   better   if   you   try."

I'm going to get up tomorrow
& do those dishes. I promise.

I'm going to scrub the floors
& answer the doorbell when it chimes.

I'm going to treat you better
& I'm going to smile.
For a while.

"I can't live with so much hate. I can't."

Neither can I.

"No one wants to hear about the bad. About the things eating you up inside. They ask how you're doing and expect to hear 'Good' or 'Fine'. And those words can never sum up exactly how I'm feeling."

–*Lisa Marie*

On Fathers That Leave

This is the poem where
I say I see you every time
I lock eyes with deep
brown in the mirror as
I fix my hair before work.

(But I don't.)

This is the poem where
I say it hurts that there
is a new little girl walking &
talking that shares
my last name &
maybe your smile,
the way I do.

(But it doesn't.)

This is the poem where
I say I wish you never left,
that I wonder why you love her the
way you never loved me,
that I feel an ache where a father's love
should be.

(But I forgot you long ago.)

This is the poem you will read.
The poem that will
be the only way you will ever know me.

(But we both know you never will.
That you never tried,
without resentment in your eyes.)

The Gravedigger

He was a father, a son, a husband.
He was a gravedigger.

Poisoner.

He buried the little girl living inside
of me before she had a chance to smile all of
her smiles.

He sleeps in a bed of vile denial.
His children chose new names.
They don't visit his plot.
He's six feet under & we never knew.

My closure lies with him & the soil & the
worms.
My hands are weary & I can't bring myself
to dig it up.

I just want to feel clean.

I bathed myself in salt tonight.
I am a scar, reopened.

My Galaxy is Dark

2,900 plus days,
crawling,
& laughing & fumbling
around on this earth.

I was 4'8, give or take.
stringy dark locks,
& often-skinned knees.

I had a deep scar on my thigh from my
bicycle & many others from swimming
with chicken pox.

Were most of your stars out at that age?
Mine had begun to dim.

Internal nerve damage
had started to set in.
Please don't make me put on another
puffy pink dress
& compete for
a beauty pageant crown.

Shame is sticky & it clings to
the bones of children quite quickly.
My skin was no longer my own.

I forgot it was made for arranging
dollhouse furniture,
for catching too swift lizards,
for running from that crazy
German Shepherd down the road.

Now
it was made for wishing on daisies,
for hoping memories would eventually
fade,
for growing skin so thick no one could see
the scars,

internal,
& the stars,
no longer eternal.

Girl Crush(ed)

Her mother's body is strong
& she taught her to love the bones
& flesh she was born in.
Yet she dreams of being a waif
because the boy who works at the
Town & Country Grocery down
the road always flirts with the cashier
as he bags groceries.
& that girl has a thigh gap
& blue glitter nail polish.
She thinks of her at night,
often more than the boy she
wants to kiss, & how she can
change her own face if she gets
an after school job & buys all
the pretty must-haves listed in
the Seventeen Magazine next to her bed.
She spends every lunch hour locked
in the last stall on the left with
a bologna on white with spicy mustard
& her feet crossed so they don't show
below the doors.
She thinks of the father that left her
& wonders if friendship
& an honest conversation
can take away the stale taste in her mouth.

How to Be a Victim

It's hot. It's humid.
I dress in layers.

Waterfalls of sweat
run along my spine.
The place I place my shame.
I don't want them to see. See me.

I am guilt & relief & a choking breath.
I am an ache & easily extracted smiles.

Tell me how to feel. Society?
You're quiet today.

It's strange seeing you this way.
I'm still waiting on my manual.

"How to Be a Victim."

I'm stumbling around
with missing parts,
but I'm still here.

Facades in Faces

I wear many faces.
The damaged girl Daddy ruined

near running water & a low
humming hair dryer.

Knees knelt, not in prayer,
but with begging eyes
& happy lies painted over
the grim reality of hot
Florida nights for too
many little girls.

I wear many faces.
The innocence you think
I own that is nothing
but a fantasy for men
who cannot handle
the ruin I will always
be wrapped up in.

When All the Clocks Break

I
would make a beautiful mother.

I
probably wouldn't get my child
to school on time,
& "just five more minutes"
chased by a cherub smile would
surely sway me at ten past nine.

I'd
wager a guess
curfews would be broken.

I
bet neon numbers would
keep me company as I stayed awake,
my fingers grazing lace window
shades with my breath held
in wait of
headlights circling in.

I
would have made a beautiful mother.
That's what they say.

I
smile & nod & say "maybe someday"
because that lie tastes sweeter.

When all the clocks break inside of me
it seems my face stays the same.

Resident Evil

There is a dark thing
that resides inside of me.

I feel it cawing in my belly.
I shudder as its wings
crawl up my throat.

It rattles my ribcage.
It never sleeps.

Its whispers cannot be
contained by the bony
cell I have sentenced it to.

Dark confessions
darken my eyes.
I feed it my lies.

"I'm fine."

"Anxiety is like torture. You have no control over what's happening and why you feel a certain way, but not everyone understands that. My question to people who do not get my behavior is, if I could stop being this way whenever I wanted, why would I repeatedly put myself through this in the first place?"

–Tanisha Jain

Parts, Pieces

I have all my parts.
Thighs,
hipbones,
ribs,
a naked neck.

I have these parts,
begging for your mouth.

I am a woman needing warmth.
Press the right buttons
& I can dance for you.

I have all my parts.
It's this suffocation that lives within,
preventing me from pushing off the bed,
as you trail your tongue along each peak of
me.

I fear the dirt within.
I'm not allowed to cry out as I am released.
I can't tell the difference in each caress.

Are you a man who loves me?
Or are you a thief like him?

Hysterical Hysterectomy

Please use a knife with a clean edge
when you slit my smooth belly open.
Take extra care when removing everything
that makes me a woman.

I am a barren womb
& a selfish grin, to you.

I'll wear that weak smirk,
steady, as you
dismember me slowly
with your words
& your worn sideways glances.

I am nothing more than a
waste of space left on the shelf.

& you are nothing more than
the judgment
my mother always
told me never to use.

Misplaced

I've convinced myself that
love will never work out for me.
Not because I cannot find a
man to love me,
but because I cannot love
the right ones in return.

Unrequited is my drink of choice.

I choose to latch onto those
who I know will not be able to say
it back, or feel it the way I do.

My grandmother told me to always be with
someone who loves more,
& I keep failing at that.
I am always looking for the one who will
destroy me.

What do I know of a pure,
constant, everlasting love from a man?
My biological father left me
before I had a chance to
even form a memory of him.

The father who raised me
ruined me & blackened

my mind with memories suppressed.

Intimacy is out of the question.
First times require shots.
I jumped ship twice
when the threat of a ring hopped on board.
I always have one hand on the ledge.

& if you won't push me I'll find
an excuse
to let go.

House Party

Sleep & I wouldn't have
each other last night.
Instead I partied with Truth, but he wouldn't
leave much for my lips.

I sat by his side, watching him sway,
vomiting out all
the things I've been choking on.
I kept quiet & held his
goddamn hair while

Silence & Guilt fucked in the corner.
As usual, they were gone this morning
but their scent still lingers.

I wonder when they will come
back for me.
Breakfast
I had broken glass for
breakfast this morning;
 I bled,
 serves me right

my mouth has been tearing you
apart for years now;
the way I speak,
  vehement

your tender eyes are too big for
your head & I love them so;
       mostly the way they smile

so, I punish myself from time to time

not for loving you
    but
for keeping you

The Con in the Inconsistent

I am nothing more than a con artist

stuffing my pretty
petal body into a
push up bra.

Painting my pretty
& smooth face with
new concealer & rouge.

Hiding my crazy neurosis
behind a laugh
& a smile that
will surely fade.

Let me scam you into loving me.
Let me lie to you
& tell you
I am everything
you have been searching for.

Let me sharpen my
teeth on your own transgressions,
the ones you aim to douse me in.
Light me up.
Undress me in
this bachelor pad.

The art by the guest bedroom,
territory markings
from your finest casualties.

Tell me what she did wrong
so I can play the part.

I don't want tomorrow
to frame us into
believing I'm the
one you need to change you.

That role belongs to the sane.

I'll try not to get off on
the longing I left on the nightstand.

Another Morning Manic

Another morning sick as a dog.
Another morning with a jackhammer
in my skull.
pounding,
raging,
never fading.

Another morning erasing texts from
the night before without a second glance.

Another morning tripping over last
night's heels
& lace & cheap gold earrings.

It seems,

the planet will continue to move
while I sift slowly through the rubble
I have become.

Swimming Like a Cinder Block

In my dreams
the past two nights,
I had a teal tail & I was friends
with a couple of clownfish.
I had an Ariel voice & a half moon smile.
I had a laugh in my throat & a dance in my
hands.

In my dreams the past two nights,
I did not fear depths.

In my bed the past two days,
I have remained.

Swimming like a cinder block
in salt stained sheets
waiting for Midas
to touch me.

Waiting for the sun
to break through the
my waves.

Bare & Unbalanced

There was an ocean on my pillow;
the night I dripped confessions
into your cupped hands still stains us.

"It was him.
A stand-in father, a thief,
with my innocence tarnished & veins
hollow."

My burden should have
been easier to bear.
I was bare & unbalanced, then.

Your touch triggered.
His acid still lingered.

You drew shutters over your eyes, a reflex.
So I screamed at your embrace, a reject.
Voiceless tombs, our four post.

"Don't touch me."

We drifted with barriers between us,
no salvation for my damned heart,
not as you dreamed.

"Is it necessary to let all this out to finally break through? To hurt the people around me in order to free myself? Or can I just let it go on my own somehow?"

–*Bianca Lupo*

Lucky 13

1

I hope you know you can't give her back her
virginity, or the innocence you stole when
you fucked another girl just one week later.

2

With her you were 'slumming it,' that was
never lost on her, in case you didn't know.

3

She never got your last name & she cried the
next day through her shift & through lunch,
all vodka & salt & hoping her mother
wouldn't call.

4

She still isn't sure if it was rape, she freezes
when she hears your name.

5

You married the other woman, she is still
laughing at you.

6

She bloodied your bed so you bloodied her
heart, now it stops & starts for no one but
you & the rest she will pretend with.

7
You "ghosted" her before it was the "in"
thing to do.

8-12
Cheap beer & charming boys.

13
She had to fight you off yet still loves your
smile; you're a card trick she will never be
able to figure out.

Sundowns in Seattle

Alva is restless.
She is restless on Tuesdays

& most Sundays.
She is restless at night,
she doesn't know my name anymore.
(I know she wants to know
my name.)

I often find her fumbling for
the letters in the bottom
drawer that sits in the corner.
Empty hands always forfeit the fight
behind her eyes.

Alva loves
Of Mice And Men
& sometimes
I read to her.
It quiets her
when the sky closes
its eyes.

She watches the day die
from her rocker in the
window.
I watch her

die a little each
day hoping she

doesn't
feel me cry.

Weltschmerz

On Grand Street there is a small alley
I pass on my way to the
Farmers Market on Saturdays.

Cecilia lives there.
Her ruby hat & plum scarf
      always catch my eye.
           So does her smile.
I bring her peaches
& quiet conversation
when my arms & mouth can manage it.

I bring her a smile of my own
when my heart can manage it.

She tells me every day she is in love
          with the world.
I ask myself every day
what the rest of us
are doing wrong.

Fools & Magicians

You're a wife. You're not allowed to frown
now. Matching bands on hands banished it
all, right? "I just want to be happy," you say

as he sips his black coffee. *As you spoon
sugar into your wounds.* Matching last
names on address labels, too cute, your

sobfest in the laundry room late last week,
let it go. He vowed to love you no matter
what, Dear, he must not know the woman

you'll become. He must not know he signed
up for war. You're the tip & he is the sheath.
You cry over a phantom who never

ever loved you & he never cries over the
smallness you have sworn as a second skin.
Can you turn your pain into a thin-tipped

arrow? To slip between his beautiful bones,
to spill out all that you pretend he is? You
miss the way your words sounded when

you would lie face down on your too soft
mattress in your tiny blue bedroom. You
traced novels on his spine, & his skin

was yours, even after your heart had
strayed. You would sigh, & he would
smile. You would whimper, & he would

draw close again. You didn't have enough
moments like that, & it buried you.
Now, they're all he remembers. You don't

recognize him these days. He is everything
you begged for, you're too scared to reach
for him. You're too scared you're a

fool & he is a magician. His skeleton
fairytale calls to you. Maybe soon you can
mold yourself into what he loves.

Risk & Roulette

Locked. Loaded.
What about the time I took
that stranger home from the bar?
I fucked his last name out of my head
& I   wanted   it.

Spin the chamber.
What about the time my high school
crush found me one Halloween night
dressed as the Devil & led
me down the jet black downtown streets
to his nearby sheets
& I   wanted   it?

Spin the chamber.
What about the time I met a man online?
He tried to take it too far
on that shitty ass couch in my dark living
room
& after five or six rejections he finally
(thankfully) left because
I   didn't   want   it.

Spin the chamber.
What about the time the bully from the
bus found me irresistible as an adult?
He fed me five more shots

& he convinced me
I   wanted   it.

I think
I've spent too many years
playing Russian Roulette
with my body in a world
already holding cold steel
to my temple.